Mel Bay Presents

Melodic Studies

& Compositions for Guitar

A Reading Workout for Serious Musicians

by Fred Hamilton

Cover Photo by Charles Baxter Photography.

"The Freddy" guitar on cover by luthier Ed Schaefer.

1 2 3 4 5 6 7 8 9 0

Visit us on the Web at www.melbay.com — E-mail us at email@melbay.com

Table of Contents

Appendix One: The Basics of Music Theory 68

Appendix Two: Rhythm Exercises 74

About the Author 90

Discography...91

Introduction

The ability to read music is an extremely valuable tool. My career as a player and teacher is, in part, due to my ability to read music well. Musical Theatre, shows, big bands, backing guest artists, jazz gigs and concerts usually call for readers. I can give you several examples of recent gigs that reading played a significant part. At the time of this writing, I am playing in the pit orchestra for Leonard Bernstein's classic musical, <u>West Side Story</u>. It is very difficult, and there was little time for advance practice. Another time I was called to perform with pianist Art Lande at a jazz club in Houston. There was a short rehearsal and all the music was original compositions by members of the band. I had to be able to read it and play it stylistically accurate with no practice time. In June 2001, I was hired to play a concert in Dallas with the great saxophonist Joe Lovano. The gig was at 8:00 and the rehearsal was immediately before from 5:00-7:00. Joe brought a stack of his original compositions, some of which were made famous by his collaboration with John Scofield. Before the rehearsal, I remember him saying something to the effect of, "I brought some music, but if reading is a problem, we can just play standards." Now, there is certainly nothing wrong with playing jazz standards, but I would have been very embarrassed if I would have had to decline to play his music because I couldn't read.

As a college professor, I have taught many guitar students in the last twenty-five years, and I know that those who were at least moderately able to read music had a much easier time in academic music classes such as theory, counterpoint, harmony and arranging. At the University of North Texas, students may not be placed in any ensembles if the ability to read music is not at the level of other more prepared students. Aside from enhancing employment and educational opportunities, I often think of simply how much pleasure I derive from playing beautiful music available only in traditional staff notation.

This book is a collection of melodic studies and compositions. It is divided into three parts. The first is intended for reading up and down the neck, horizontally on each single string. Mick Goodrick calls this "The Science of the Unitar" in his book, *The Advancing Guitarist*. I have written numerous studies that will help you see each string in a more stepwise, piano-like manner and facilitate logical shifts. Part Two is made up of studies to be played in position across the neck. Each position has a range of two-octaves and a fourth. Part Three is a collection of longer compositions that give you the opportunity to work out fingerings around the neck on your own. In the appendix section of the book, there are some theory and reading tips and rhythmic exercises. You may need some preparation, if so, work through these prior to beginning the studies.

I know of no shortcut to develop reading skills. A daily commitment to reading music during your practice time is the only way to get better. I have written this book with that in mind. Work slowly, be patient and listen. The music is challenging, persevere with the goal of accurately playing each study at the suggested tempo before moving to the next.

PART ONE
Horizontal Studies

When you look at the piano keyboard, every octave is the same. You see the half steps and the intervals very clearly. The guitar can be viewed in the same manner, if you approach each string as its own instrument. The steps up and down the neck are logical and visible much like the piano keyboard. Adjacent frets are a half-step apart, also called a minor second. The chromatic scale is made up of half-steps or minor seconds. A whole-step, a major second, is two frets up or down. The major scale is made up of combinations of whole- and half-steps. The white keys on a piano illustrate this. Two whole-steps, half-step, three whole-steps and a half-step make the one-octave major scale. Larger intervals are longer distances. The beginning of "The Star Spangled Banner" is composed using one minor third and a major third, which yields a major triad. On the guitar, an interval of a minor third on the same string covers the distance of three frets, which would be from the first to the fourth finger if each finger occupies one fret as a position. A major third is a stretch of four frets. The following studies will require you to frequently shift up and down the neck. Keep all the fingers close to the neck, avoiding lifting them too high. When you shift, a smooth, fast and precise hand movement is necessary to produce long, legato sounds. Legendary jazz guitarist Johnny Smith advised when possible to keep a finger **touching** the string as you shift, kind of like sliding into the next position, as opposed to lifting all the fingers off the neck. You must do it quickly and efficiently so that the slide, also called a glissando, will not be audible.

Horizontal Chromatic Scales

Play the scales very slowly, in time, and say the name of each note aloud.
When a sharp or flat precedes the note, say F♯ or G♭.

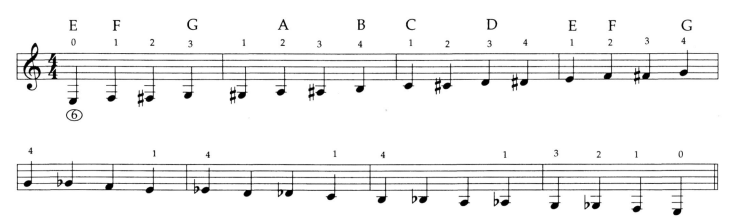

Note: When you shift up or down to the next four-finger position,
move the hand quickly, keeping all the fingers very close to the board.
The first finger should feel like it is sliding on the string, but not audible.

Same Fingering for Each String

Chromatic Scale Exercise

It is very important to count aloud when beginning each exercise. Don't depend upon feel or luck, counting is absolutely essential. The rhythms in this excercise incorporate half notes, quarter notes, eighth notes, triplets and some syncopation. When counting the triplet, you can use the syllables "trip-a-let"" to define the three notes that fit into one beat for the eighth note triplet.

Remember to shift smoothly up and down the neck, keep the fingers as close to the neck as possible. When you shift, try to imagine the neck being slippery and you are skating or sliding to the next group of notes. In these exercises, the Roman numerals will remind you of which fret a particular note is found.

A string

m.m. ♩ = 108

low E string

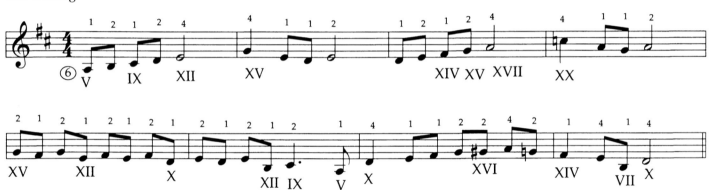

A Modal Melody Fingered Horizontally

m.m. ♩ = 120

If necessary, write fingering and fret numbers

The following phrases are identical and fingered the same, but played on the next adjacent string for each key change.

Since most notes can be fingered in several different locations and string combinations, be aware of your options so that a passage can be fingered in the most logical, stylistic and comfortable way possible. Watch the fingering and string numbers carefully. The goal of the exercise is to quickly see where the notes of a phrase could be fingered on a different string. The written fingerings are not the only available choices. Try others after you have learned these.

This is another exercise using fingering options around the neck. Pay attention to fingering, string numbers and fret numbers. Remember, the ♮ sign moves the note from its' key signature location for the duration of that measure only, or until it is changed in the measure.

15

1

Notice that the melody from measure #1-16 is identical to the melody from measure #17-32, two octaves apart. The rest of the exercise utilizes fragments of the melody, switching back and forth from the first to the sixth strings.

♩ = 100   Swing the eighth notes

2

3

♩ = 132   Medium Swing Feel

4

♩ = 144   Straight eighth note rock feel, the notes marked with a ">" above them should receive an accent with the pick.

5

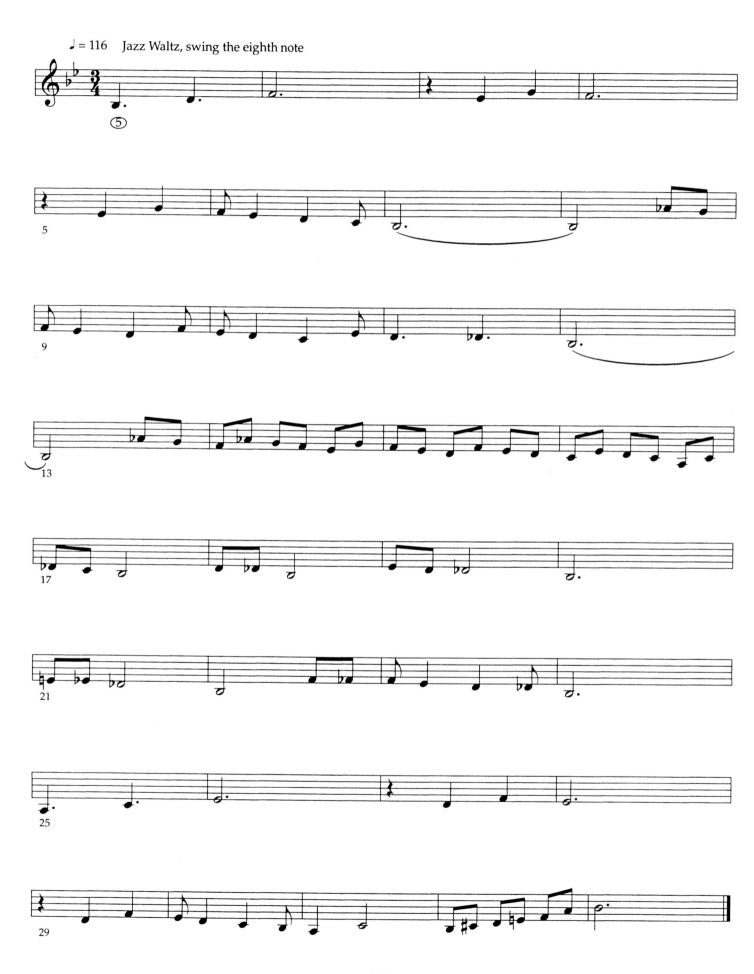

6

This might seem fast for shifting up and down one string, but have you ever heard a sitar? Indian classical music is a beautiful sound, and Ravi Shankar was very influential to me as a young guitarist. When I saw him play, I realized he very often moved up and down the neck playing melodies on one or two strings in a horizontal manner. It is a very legato and liquid style.

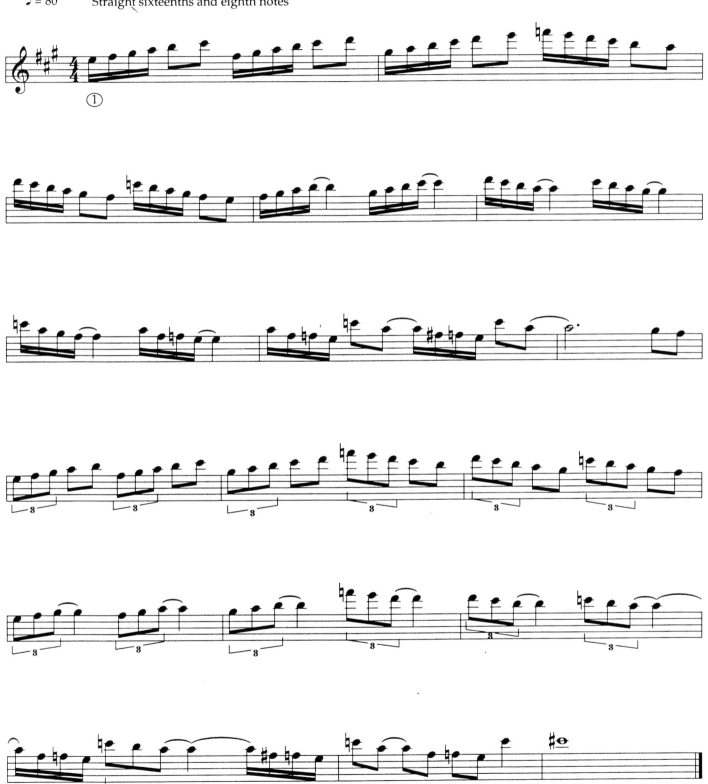

7

The time signature "12/8" is a typical way of notating a slow blues feel. It really gets four counts per measure, but each beat is divided into three, like a triplet. The three eighth notes are normally beamed together. When you see a quarter note followed by an eighth note, keep the feeling of three in mind and place the eighth note on the third note of the beat. That should give it the feeling of a slow swing.

8

Bebop tempo, swing eighth notes. Cut time should be felt with two beats for each measure. Try using a metronome set at the tempo marking, feeling the time in two with the beats on two and four like the hi hat in a drum set.

9

In this study, there are slur marks. These are the curved lines like you have seen tying two notes together. When placed to a different note, you will either hammer-on or pull-off. Pick the first note, if the next note is higher in pitch, you must quickly and forcefully place the appropriate left hand finger down on the new note. If it is lower in pitch, you pick the first and then pull the string as you lift your finger to allow the new note to sound. This is a great way to produce a more lyrical, singing quality. It sounds more like a horn player or singer would phrase using breath to move to a new note.

10

Instead of writing out an identical phrase, often there will be repeat signs in the music. Go back to the previous repeat sign and play that section again. Unless marked otherwise it will only be repeated once. The time signature "7/4" can be counted and felt as a combination of 4/4 + 3/4 or 3/4 + 4/4. This etude should be counted and felt as 4/4 + 3/4.

♩ = 176   Calypso Feel

11

A repeat will sometimes have a different way of ending the phrase than the original, so a first and second ending is utilized. You read into the first ending, then repeat back to the repeat sign. On the second time playing the passage, you read into the second ending and skip the measures in the first ending. You then continue reading into the new section.

Remember, the ">" above a note designates a stronger accent giving the note its' full value. The accent that looks like a pyramid or a teepee(^) calls for the note to be shorter in length than notated. Use all down strokes for this study. Try muting the string with the palm of the right hand. When you have it down, add the fifth above each eighth note and quarter note for "power chords".

12

The notes will remain on the string previously notated until a new string number appears. This study has large amounts of space notated by rests. Rests are very important and also easy to rush through. To avoid coming in early or late, count aloud. Give them the exact amount of space. Don't rush through. Silence frames the sound. Pay attention to the fingerings. Write in fret numbers, if necessary.

27

PART TWO
Position Studies

These exercises are written to explore fingerings across the neck. When you put your left hand on a particular string, each finger is placed on a fret. The fret that the first finger occupies will be assigned a Roman numeral, which designates the position. Some of the notes will be fingered by moving the first finger back or the fourth finger up the neck one fret. So, the complete position really covers six frets when you stretch the hand out. Since you have finished the horizontal studies, the linear aspect of each string should be easier to see and understand. By limiting yourself to particular positions, you will see and feel the neck in a totally different perspective. The key in both ways of playing is in the limitation. Eliminating our singular view of the neck and opening up new routes and pathways to get from note to note. Different tone quality and phrasing is often the result.

Reading in Position

The tempo on these short positional studies should be as slow as is necessary to play correctly. Increase the tempo after it has been learned slowly. Use a metronome as soon as you can negotiate the notes.

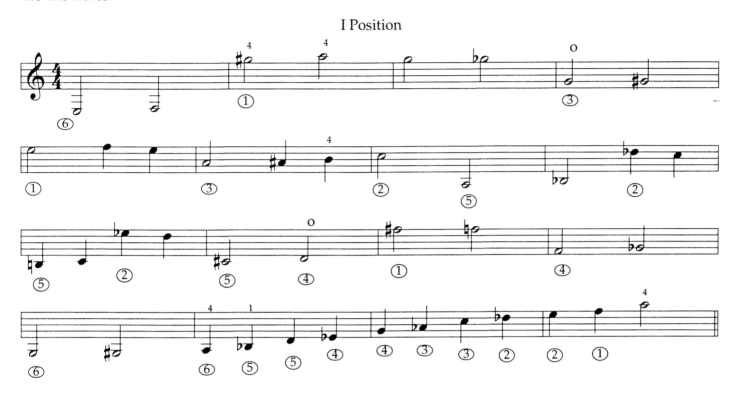

Learn this first with the open strings, then practice fingering the fifth fret notes, which, except for B, are the open strings (A, D, G, E)

I Position

This is the same exercise transposed to G♭ major, finger it in first position.

I Position

II Position

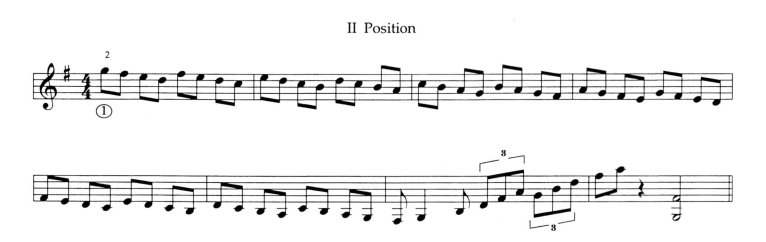

II Position

III Position

III Position

III Position

IV Position

IV Position

V Position

VI Position

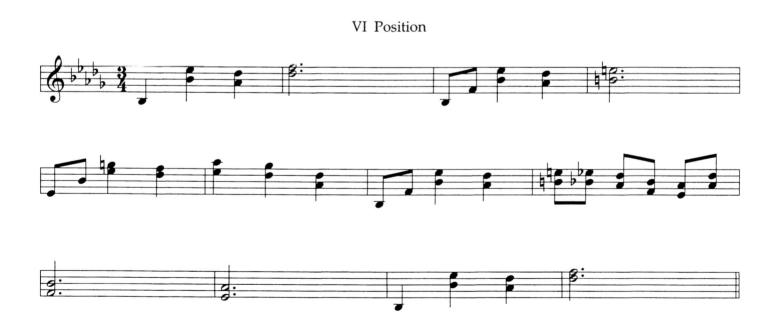

VI Position

VII Position

VII Position

VIII Position

VIII Position

IX Position

The time signature of 9/8 may be counted in two ways. You can count nine beats per measure with the eighth note as one beat, or you can count it in three with the dotted quarter (three eighths) receiving one beat.

IX Position

X Position

X Position

XI Position

XI Position

XII Position

40

1

I Position (use open strings)

2

Latin-Funk Feel

♩ = 88   two beats per measure

II Position

3

III Position

4

IV Position

x=double sharp

5

V Position

6

♩ = 200

VI Position

7

8

9

10

11

12

PART THREE
Extended Compositions

You have now read and learned a lot of music and forced yourself to learn fingerings that were perhaps unusual. In this part of the book, I have composed complete pieces of music for you to make fingering decisions. If necessary, mark fingerings, string numbers or fret numbers to give yourself consistency from day to day as you practice the piece. Try passages up the neck, across the neck or in combinations. Since the music is composed with guitar in mind, there will be ways that should feel more natural and easier to accomplish. Don't always go with the first fingerings you hit upon. You may need to rethink strategies if something does not feel good.

Blues Dues

Dancing With the Monk

This page has been left blank
to avoid awkward page turns.

Three Jitterbugs

A Balinese Puppet Show

Raga Rishy

A raga is an improvised performance upon a specified group of notes. Although this composition is only an image of the style, it does make use of three contrasting sections in a raga called the alap, the jor and the jhala. The first, from measures 1-12 is a short alap defining the scale (Major without a 6th: 1, 2, 3, 4, 5, 7) and can be played loosely without adhering to the metronomic consistency of time. The jor, at measure 13 is where the consistent time begins in a slow 7/4 groove. The jhala begins at measure 44, the eighth note of the slow 7/4 becomes the main unit of time in the doubled 7/8 groove. This is where the tabla (North Indian hand drum) would enter. It should "burn".

Indian classical music utilizes a drone. Let each low E sound throughout the phrase. You may resound the E whenever you want to reinforce the drone within the composition. Sitar and sarod players commonly use horizontal fingering. This is a good piece to practice Part One of this book.

Play the written notes on the G string, play open B and E with each written note.

Play the written notes on the G string, play open B and E with each written note.

APPENDIX ONE
The Basics of Music Theory

This is not a complete treatise on music theory. I have included this section to give you some basics in case you need review before beginning the musical studies in this book. Here are a few Mel Bay titles for further study on music theory:

95736 Encyclopedia of Scales, Modes, and Melodic Patterns
96206BCD Complete Book of Harmony, Theory, and Voicings for Guitar
95112 Complete Book of Harmony, Theory, and Voicings for Guitar
98287 Understanding How to Build Guitar Chords and Arpeggios

The Basics of Music Theory

Music notation is a way to graph sound. Pitch is visually represented as an eliptical shape called a note, which is placed on a line or space of the staff. The staff is a group of five lines. At the beginning of a staff of music there will be a symbol called a clef. It specifies the letter names and the sound that will be assoiciated with that clef. The two most common are treble and bass clef. Guitar will normally read in treble clef.

The Staff

treble clef

The treble clef curls around the G line.

Each line and space is a designation for a pitch.
An easy way to rememger the lines is the phrase
"EVERY GOOD BOY DOES FINE."
The note names of the spaces spell the word "FACE."
The musical alphabet only uses the letters A-G.

Ledger Lines

When the notes are written above or below the staff, the extra lines are called "ledger lines," and the alphabet continues, one letter at a time.

Time Signatures

The top number notates how many beats are in each measure. The bottom number refers to the unit receiving one beat. In these time signatures, the quarter note receives one beat. The most common are 4/4 and 3/4.

In these time signatures, the eighth note receives one beat.

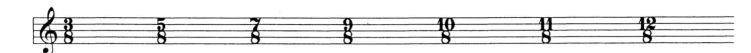

This time signature is an abbreviation for 2/2, and is called Cut Time. Each measure looks like 4/4 but is counted with two beats per measure. It is a very common designation for fast tempos.

Rhythmic Notation

Music occupies time and to notate that, notes are represented in different ways. Whole and half notes are not filled in. A whole note receives four beats, half notes get two .

Dotted Notes

When a dot is placed after a note, half of its normal value is added to it.

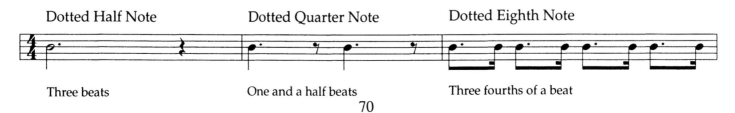

70

Triplets

Three notes beamed together with the numeral 3 above them are called triplets and occupy the space of two of the normal rhythmic units. If the triplet is made of quarter notes, three quarters will be evenly played in the space of two normal quarter notes. Similarly, three eighth notes or three sixteenth notes will occupy the space of two.

Rests

Music must have space and that is designated with symbols in the staff that correspond to rhythmic units of time. Whole, half, quarter, eighth and sixteenth note rests are counted just as if you were playing the note, but instead there is silence. When a dot is placed after the rest it lengthens it by half of its value, just as a dotted note.

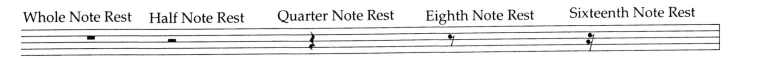

Ties and Slurs

The curved line that is found between two notes of the same pitch is called a tie. As the word implies, it ties two notes together. Pick the first note and let it ring through the duration of the next note. It is like counting a rest, only the original note rings through. When the curved line connects two notes of different pitch, it is called a slur. On the guitar, this will usually denote a pull-off or a hammer-on. If the pitch is descending, pick the first note and pull the string with your left hand finger to sound the next note. When ascending, pick the first note and quickly "hammer" the appropriate finger down on the board to sound the next note. When the slur is over more than two notes, use a combination of either pull-offs or hammer-ons and light picking to produce a smooth, legato (singing) phrase.

Key Signatures

There are twelve keys, each one locating a specific home base, called the tonic. The key signature is normally associated with a major key or its relative minor. The white keys of the piano from C to C is the C major scale and all of the natural notes of the key of C, which has no sharps or flats in the key signature. Major scales are built in intervals that are mathematically defined as: two whole steps, one half step, three whole steps, one half step. C to D is a whole step with the note C♯ or D♭ between them.

A whole step is made of two half steps. A whole step is also called a major second, a half step is called a minor second. There is no note between two half steps. D to E is a whole step with D♯ or E♭ between them. E to F is a half step, with no note between them. F to G is a whole step with F♯ or G♭ between them. G to A is a whole step. A to B is a whole step. B to C is a half step. If you have never done so, look at a piano and notice the white and black key arrangements. When you change key, the mathematical interval formula stays the same, but there is a different starting place and home base, therefore sharps and flats are used to move a note up or down permanently in that key signature. The only time that a note in a key signature is played as a different pitch is when there is a ♭, ♯ or ♮ (natural) placed before the note. It will remain at that pitch only in that measure or until it is changed in that measure.

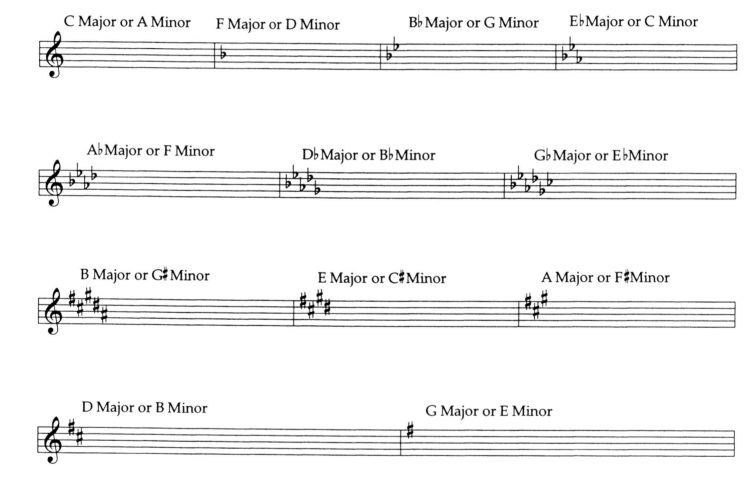

Notes on the Guitar

Open Strings

Arabic Numerals in Circles Designate the String (6 is low, 1 is high)

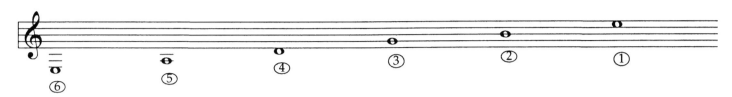

Roman Numerals Designate the Fret

APPENDIX TWO

Rhythm Exercises

Counting and understanding rhythms is really a mental discipline, unrelated to the ability to play the guitar. I have written these exercises to give you more practice in reading rhythms. Tap them out on your leg, a table, a drum, a guitar, clap or sing them. You can play them on the guitar using the designated pitch, change the pitches to relieve sonic boredom or use chords.

Rhythm Exercises

As you play these exercises, count aloud while you play. If necessary, write in the counting for the rest of the exercises as the example in the first two.

1

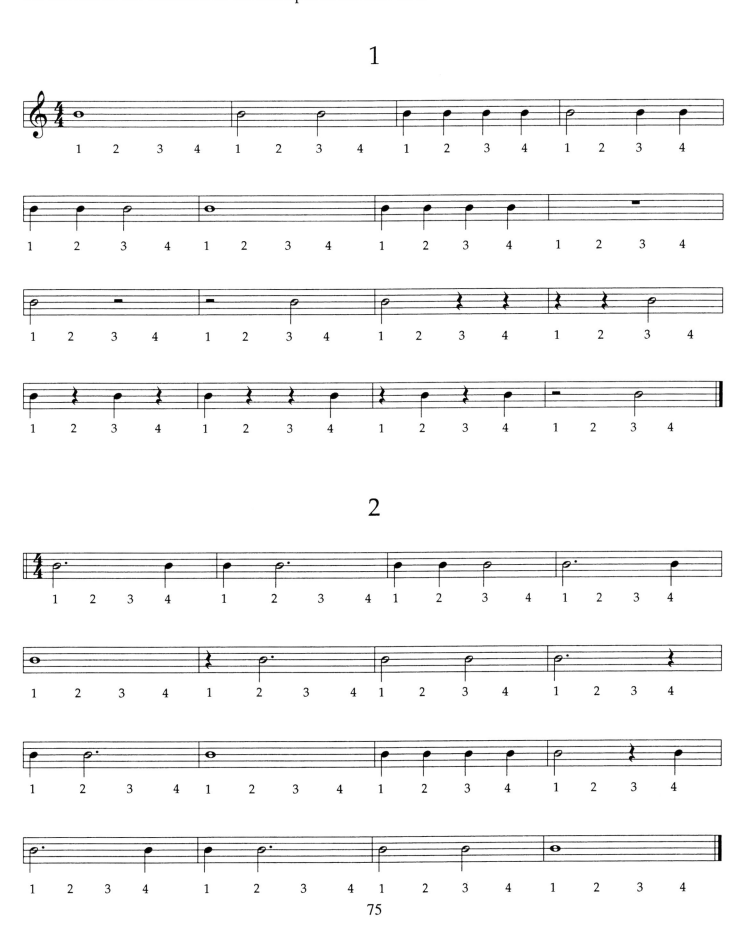

2

3

4

5

6

7

8

11

12

13

Dotted notes lengthen the original by half of the value.

1 & 2 & 3 & 4 &   1 & 2 & 3 & 4 &

When a note is "tied" to the next note, the second note is held and not picked again

14

15

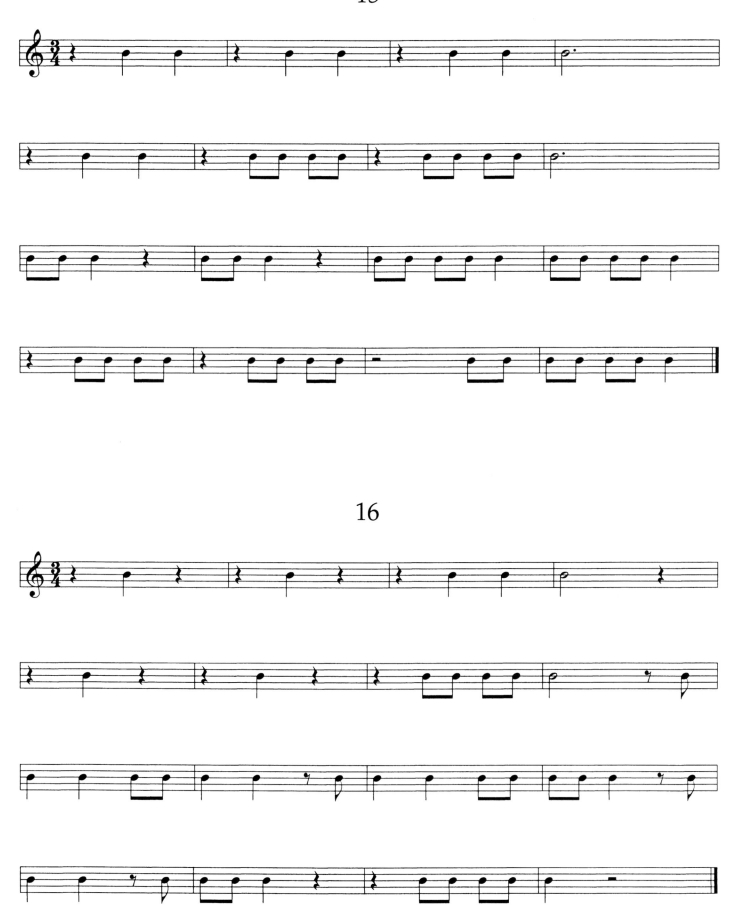

16

17

18

19

20

21

22

23

24

25

26

27

28

29

About the Author

FRED HAMILTON is a guitarist, multi-instrumentalist and a professor in the Jazz Studies Division at the University of North Texas. He teaches guitar, jazz improvisation, rhythm section master class and directs the guitar ensembles. He has played bass or guitar with Bill Frisell, Joe Lovano, Cedar Walton, Mike Stern, James Moody, George Garzone, David Liebman, Marvin Stamm, Bill Mays, Kenny Wheeler, Art Lande and many others. He is the bassist and guitarist in the Earl Harvin Trio and has toured and recorded four albums since the group's formation in 1993. He is a founding member of the group Brahma, and in it plays guitars, dobro, the Hindustani slide guitar and banjo. During the summer, Fred teaches and performs at a variety of workshops, which has included the University of Washington, the University of Colorado, the Nairopa Institute, the University of North Texas and the Jamey Aebersold Summer Jazz Workshops.

Denton, Texas and UNT have been home since 1989, and prior to that, he held positions on the faculty at Concordia College in Montreal (1984-85), St. Francis Xavier University in Nova Scotia (1982-84), and Bowling Green State University in Ohio (1979-82). He received the Bachelor and Master of Music degrees in composition from the University of Northern Colorado where he was a graduate teaching fellow from 1978 to 1979. Prior to that he played guitar and composed and arranged for the Commanders Jazz Ensemble in the U.S. Air Force with the NORAD Command Band (1972-76).

During his formative years in Denver, Colorado, he studied with Jim Atkins, original rhythm guitarist with the Les Paul Trio. The other influential guitarist in the Denver area during his youth was the legendary Johnny Smith.

Fred endorses Schaefer Guitars and Thomastik Strings. For further information, visit www.fred-hamilton.com or http://www.music.unt.edu/jazz..

Discography

Unicorporated, the Earl Harvin Trio, Two Ohm Hop (2001)
Between Us Cats, DPZ (2001)
Kenny Wheeler at North Texas, UNT Jazz (2001)
Second Wind, Pete Brewer (April, 2000)
Traveling Light, Genie Grant and Dave Zoller, DPZ (October, 1999)
Earl Harvin Trio, Live at the Gypsy Tea Room, Leaning House (June, 1999)
Rodney Booth Quartet, 1999
3x4x3, Dave Zoller, DPZ (1998)
Strange Happy, Earl Harvin Trio, Leaning House (1997)
The Earl Harvin Trio/Quartet, Leaning House (1995)
Strange Beauty, Tony Campise, Heart (1995)
Looking Back on Tomorrow, Fred Hamilton, with David Friesen
    and Ed Soph, Wolf Tales (1994)
The Three Pigs and the Billy Goats' Gruff, Art Lande, Paul McCandless and narration by
    Holly Hunter, Rabbit Ears/Windham Hill (1989)
The Odd Couple, Spike Robinson and Rob Mullins, Capri (1989)

For Information on Concepts or Workshops:
Fred Hamilton
(940) 565 3236
hamilton@music.unt.edu

EXCELLENCE IN MUSIC

MEL BAY®

Since 1947